# ACID REFLUX COOKBOOK

**MEGA BUNDLE – 4 Manuscripts in 1 – 160+ Acid Reflux - friendly recipes including casserroles, side dishes and pasta recipes**

# TABLE OF CONTENTS

is universal as so. The presentation of the information is without contract or any type of guarantee assurance.

The trademarks that are used are without any consent, and the publication of the trademark is without permission or backing by the trademark owner. All trademarks and brands within this book are for clarifying purposes only and are the owned by the owners themselves, not affiliated with this document.

Introduction

Acid Reflux recipes for personal enjoyment but also for family enjoyment. You will love them for sure for how easy it is to prepare them.

## ROASTED ALMONDS

| | |
|---|---|
| Serves: | **3-4** |
| Prep Time: | **10** Minutes |
| Cook Time: | **20** Minutes |
| Total Time: | **30** Minutes |

### INGREDIENTS

- 1 lb. almonds
- 2 tablespoons olive oil
- 1 tsp curry powder
- 1 tsp salt

### DIRECTIONS

1. Preheat the oven to 400 F
2. Cut everything in half lengthwise
3. Toss everything with olive oil and place onto a prepared baking sheet
4. Roast for 18-20 minutes at 400 F or until golden brown
5. When ready remove from the oven and serve

Serves:        **3-4**
Prep Time:   **10**   Minutes

Cook Time:  **20**   Minutes

Total Time:  **30**   Minutes

## INGREDIENTS

- 2 delicata squashes
- 2 tablespoons olive oil
- 1 tsp curry powder
- 1 tsp salt

## DIRECTIONS

1. Preheat the oven to 400 F
2. Cut everything in half lengthwise
3. Toss everything with olive oil and place onto a prepared baking sheet
4. Roast for 18-20 minutes at 400 F or until golden brown
5. When ready remove from the oven and serve

# SOUP RECIPES

## ZUCCHINI SOUP

Serves: **4**

Prep Time: **10** Minutes

Cook Time: **20** Minutes

Total Time: **30** Minutes

### INGREDIENTS

- 1 tablespoon olive oil
- 1 lb. zucchini
- ¼ red onion
- ½ cup all-purpose flour
- ¼ tsp salt
- ¼ tsp pepper
- 1 can vegetable broth
- 1 cup heavy cream

### DIRECTIONS

1. In a saucepan heat olive oil and sauté zucchini until tender
2. Add remaining ingredients to the saucepan and bring to a boil
3. When all the vegetables are tender transfer to a blender and blend until smooth
4. Pour soup into bowls, garnish with parsley and serve

## CHICKEN WITH CAULIFLOWER AND OLIVES

Serves:          **4**
Prep Time:    **10**   Minutes

Cook Time:   **60**   Minutes

Total Time:   **70**   Minutes

### INGREDIENTS

- 1 bouquet thyme
- 1 head cauliflower
- ½ cup lemon juice
- 1 lb chicken breast
- 3 ½ tbs olive oil
- 1 ½ cup olives
- 4 cloves garlic
- 1 shallot
- 1 tsp salt
- 1 ½ tsp pepper
- ½ lemon zest

### DIRECTIONS

1. Rinse the chicken breast and pat dry.
2. Spread the thyme springs in a baking dish.

3. Place the chicken over and add the cauliflower.
4. Mix the olive oil, olives, pepper, shallot, lemon juice and zest, garlic and salt.
5. Pour the mixture over the chicken.
6. Refrigerate overnight.
7. Bake at 400 for 1 hour.

| Serves: | **4** | |
|---|---|---|
| Prep Time: | **130** | Minutes |
| Cook Time: | **20** | Minutes |
| Total Time: | **150** | Minutes |

## INGREDIENTS

- 3 cloves garlic
- ½ cup lemon juice
- 1 tsp salt
- 3 tbs oil
- 1 lb chicken breast
- ½ cup rosemary

## DIRECTIONS

1. Mix the lemon juice, oil, rosemary, salt and garlic.
2. Rinse the chicken breast and pat dry.
3. Place the chicken breast in a baking dish.
4. Pour the mixture over and refrigerate for 2-3 hours.
5. Grill the chicken for 6 minutes on each side.

# SALMON BURGERS

Serves:      *12*

Prep Time:   *10*   Minutes

Cook Time:   *30*   Minutes

Total Time:   *40*   Minutes

## INGREDIENTS

- 3 eggs
- 2 tbs flour
- ½ cup sesame seeds
- 4 tbs oil
- 2 tbs vinegar
- 2 cloves garlic
- 1 lb salmon
- 2 tsp ginger
- ½ cup scallions

## DIRECTIONS

1. Rinse the salmon and pat dry.
2. Cut into cubes.
3. Mix the eggs, vinegar, scallions, 2 tbs oil, ginger, sesame seeds and ginger.
4. Add the salmon, then stir in the flour.
5. Form the mixture into patties.

6. Heat the rest of the oil in a frying pan.
7. Cook the patties for 5 minutes on each side.
8. Serve immediately.

Serves:          **2**

Prep Time:    **5**    Minutes

Cook Time:   **5**    Minutes

Total Time:   **10**   Minutes

## INGREDIENTS

- ½ tsp salt
- 4 cucumbers
- 3 tbs oil
- 6 ounces argula
- 2 tbs lemon juice

## DIRECTIONS

1. Mix the ingredients in a large bowl.
2. Serve when ready

Serves: **4**

Prep Time: **10** Minutes

Cook Time: **30** Minutes

Total Time: **40** Minutes

## INGREDIENTS

- 1 ½ cups tomato puree
- 1 ½ tbs lime juice
- 1 ½ tsp oil
- 1 lb turkey
- 1 avocado
- 1 onion
- 1 red pepper
- 3 tsp chile powder
- 1 ½ tsp oregano
- ½ tsp garlic
- 2 tsp garlic
- 2 tsp cumin

## DIRECTIONS

1. Mash the avocado, then add the lime juice and garlic and mix.
2. Heat the oil in a pan, then add the red pepper and onions and saute.

3. Add ground turkey.
4. Add the cumin, oregano, garlic and chile powder.
5. Add the tomato puree after the turkey is well cooked and simmer for a little.
6. Fill the lettuce cups with the meat mixture and serve.

Serves:        *2*
Prep Time:    *10*  Minutes

Cook Time:    *15*  Minutes

Total Time:   *25*  Minutes

## INGREDIENTS

- 2 eggs
- 2 tbs cheese
- 2 pieces bacon
- 1 avocado
- 1 tsp salt

## DIRECTIONS

1. Preheat the oven to 425F.
2. Cut the avocado in half.
3. Scoop out some of the avocado.
4. Crack the egg inside the avocado.
5. Sprinkle some cheese and salt on top, then top with bacon.
6. Cook for 15 minutes.
7. Serve warm.

# EGGS BAKED IN MUSHROOMS

Serves: **2**

Prep Time: **10** Minutes

Cook Time: **20** Minutes

Total Time: **30** Minutes

## INGREDIENTS

- 4 mushrooms
- 1 tsp black pepper
- 4 eggs
- 3 tbs cheese
- 3 tbs parsley
- 1 tsp garlic powder
- 2 tbs oil
- 1 tsp salt

## DIRECTIONS

1. Preheat the broiler.
2. Line a baking sheet.
3. Season the mushrooms with the oil, ½ tsp salt, ½ tsp pepper and ½ tsp garlic powder.
4. Broil for 5 minutes on each side.
5. Remove from oven then set the temperature to 400.
6. Crack an egg into each mushroom.

7. Sprinkle some cheese on top, then bake for 15 minutes.

8. Sprinkle with the remaining seasonings and garnish with parsley, then serve.

# TURMERIC CAULIFLOWER

Serves: **4**

Prep Time: **10** Minutes

Cook Time: **20** Minutes

Total Time: **30** Minutes

## INGREDIENTS

- 1 cauliflower
- 1 tsp black pepper
- 4 tbs oil
- 2 tsp turmeric
- 2 tsp salt
- 1 tsp garlic powder
- 2 tbs oregano

## DIRECTIONS

1. Preheat the oven to 400F.
2. Chop the cauliflower.
3. Pour the oil over it.
4. Sprinkle the remaining ingredients over.
5. Bake for 20 minutes.

Serves:        **4**
Prep Time:     **10**   Minutes

Cook Time:     **20**   Minutes

Total Time:    **10**   Minutes

## INGREDIENTS

-   1 cup quinoa
-   ½ cup cranberries
-   3 tsp olive oil
-   ½ onion
-   1 bunch of kale
-   2 tsp salt
-   1 ½ tsp black pepper
-   1 cup feta
-   ½ cup almonds
-   3 tsp lemon juice

## DIRECTIONS

1.  Cook the quinoa for 15 minutes in boiling salted water.
2.  Drain in a sieve, then add the cranberries, cover and set aside.
3.  Heat 1 ½ tsp oil and saute the onion.
4.  Add the kale and cook for 5 minutes.
5.  Season with salt.

6. Add the kale to quinoa, along with the feta and almonds and the lemon juice.

Serves:        **4**
Prep Time:   **20**   Minutes

Cook Time:  **75**   Minutes

Total Time:  **95**   Minutes

## INGREDIENTS

- 1 egg
- 2 cups ketchup
- ½ cup bread crumbs
- 3 tbs soy sauce
- 2 ½ tsp basil
- 1 ½ tsp garlic powder
- ½ cup parsley
- 2 lb ground turkey
- ½ cup cheese
- 1 ½ tbs oregano
- 4 tbs Worcestershire sauce
- ½ cup oats

## DIRECTIONS

1. Preheat the oven to 400F.
2. Mix together all of the ingredients until combined.

3. Form the mixture into a loaf shape.
4. Top with ketchup.
5. Bake for 75 minutes.

Serves: **4**
Prep Time: **20** Minutes

Cook Time: **25** Minutes

Total Time: **45** Minutes

## INGREDIENTS

- 1 ½ tsp vinegar
- 1 9-ounce can tomato sauce
- 8 hamburger buns
- 1 carrot
- 10 ounces ground beef
- 2 tsp garlic powder
- 1 ½ tsp chili powder
- ½ tsp black pepper
- ½ cup ketchup
- 1 tbs mustard
- 1 ½ tbs Worcestershire sauce
- 1 tbs tomato paste
- 1 cup onion

## DIRECTIONS

1. **Preheat the broiler.**

2. Heat a skillet.

3. Great the carrot.

4. Cook the beef, carrot, and onion for 5 minutes.

5. Add the chili powder, garlic powder and pepper, then cook for another minute.

6. Mix the ketchup, mustard, Worcestershire sauce, vinegar, tomato pasta and tomato sauce.

7. Add the mixture to the skillet.

8. Simmer for 5 minutes.

9. Toast the halved buns.

10. Place the mixture on the bottom half of the bun, then cover with the top half.

Serves:        *15*
Prep Time:   *10*   Minutes

Cook Time:   *10*   Minutes

Total Time:  *20*   Minutes

### INGREDIENTS

- 1 ½ tbs butter
- 1 cup breadcrumbs
- 1 ½ tbs yogurt
- 2 tbs green onion
- 1 10-ounces package spinach
- 1 egg
- 1 tsp paprika
- 1 cup cheese

### DIRECTIONS

1. Mix all of the ingredients in a bowl.
2. Form balls.
3. Bake at 350F for 15-20 minutes.

# GREEN PESTO PASTA

Serves:        **2**
Prep Time:     **5**    Minutes
Cook Time:     **15**   Minutes
Total Time:    **20**   Minutes

## INGREDIENTS

- 4 oz. spaghetti
- 2 cups basil leaves
- 2 garlic cloves
- ¼ cup olive oil
- 2 tablespoons parmesan cheese
- ½ tsp black pepper

## DIRECTIONS

1. Bring water to a boil and add pasta
2. In a blend add parmesan cheese, basil leaves, garlic and blend
3. Add olive oil, pepper and blend again
4. Pour pesto onto pasta and serve when ready

Serves:      **2**
Prep Time:   **5**   Minutes

Cook Time:   **5**   Minutes

Total Time:  **10**  Minutes

## INGREDIENTS

- 3 cups tomatoes
- 2 oz. mozzarella cheese
- 2 tablespoons basil
- 1 tablespoon olive oil

## DIRECTIONS

1. In a bowl combine all ingredients together and mix well
2. Serve with dressing

# BUTTERNUT SQUASH SALAD

Serves:        2
Prep Time:     5   Minutes

Cook Time:     5   Minutes

Total Time:   *10*  Minutes

## INGREDIENTS

- 3 cups butternut squash
- 1 cup cooked couscous
- 2 cups kale leaves
- 2 tablespoons cranberries
- 2 oz. goat cheese
- 1 cup salad dressing

## DIRECTIONS

1. In a bowl combine all ingredients together and mix well
2. Serve with dressing

# SALMON EGG SALAD

Serves:        **2**
Prep Time:     **5**   Minutes

Cook Time:     **5**   Minutes

Total Time:    **10**  Minutes

## INGREDIENTS

- 2 hard boiled eggs
- ¼ cup red onion
- 2 tablespoons capers
- 1 tablespoon lime juice
- 3 oz. smoked salmon
- 1 tablespoon olive oil

## DIRECTIONS

1. In a bowl combine all ingredients together and mix well
2. Serve with dressing

QUINOA SALAD

| | | |
|---|---|---|
| Serves: | **2** | |
| Prep Time: | **5** | Minutes |
| Cook Time: | **5** | Minutes |
| Total Time: | **10** | Minutes |

## INGREDIENTS

- 1 cup cooked quinoa
- 1 tablespoon olive oil
- 1 tablespoon mustard
- 2 tablespoons lemon juice
- 1 cucumber
- ½ red onion
- ½ cup almonds
- 1 tablespoon mint

## DIRECTIONS

1. In a bowl combine all ingredients together and mix well
2. Serve with dressing

# GREEK SALAD

Serves:        2

Prep Time:     5    Minutes

Cook Time:     5    Minutes

Total Time:   10    Minutes

## INGREDIENTS

- 1 cup cucumber
- ¼ cup tomatoes
- ¼ cup red onion
- ¼ cup avocado
- ¼ cup feta cheese
- 1 tablespoon olives
- ¼ pecans
- 1 tablespoon vinegar
- 1 tsp olive oil

## DIRECTIONS

1. In a bowl combine all ingredients together and mix well
2. Serve with dressing

# AVOCADO SALAD

Serves:         2
Prep Time:      5   Minutes
Cook Time:      5   Minutes
Total Time:    10   Minutes

## INGREDIENTS

- 1 cup corn
- 1 cup tomatoes
- 1 cup cucumber
- ½ cup avocado
- ½ cup edamame
- 1 cup salad dressing

## DIRECTIONS

1. In a bowl combine all ingredients together and mix well
2. Serve with dressing

# BAKED LEMON SALMON

Serves: **1**

Prep Time: **10** Minutes

Cook Time: **20** Minutes

Total Time: **30** Minutes

## INGREDIENTS

- 1 zucchini
- 1 onion
- 1 scallion
- 1 salmon fillet
- 1 tsp lemon zest
- 1 tsp olive oil
- Lemon slices

## DIRECTIONS

1. Preheat the oven to 375 F
2. In a baking dish add zucchini, onion and sprinkle vegetables with salt and lemon zest
3. Lay salmon fillet and season with salt, lemon zest and olive oil
4. Bake at 375 F for 15-18 minutes
5. When ready remove from the oven and serve with lemon slices

Serves: **1**

Prep Time: **10** Minutes

Cook Time: **10** Minutes

Total Time: **20** Minutes

## INGREDIENTS

- 1 zucchini
- ¼ tsp oregano
- Salt
- 1 cup cooked quinoa
- 1 cup spinach
- 1 cup mixed greens
- ½ cup red pepper
- ¼ cup cucumber
- ¼ cup tomatoes
- parsley
- Tahini dressing

## DIRECTIONS

1. In a skillet heat olive oil olive and sauté zucchini until soft and sprinkle oregano over zucchini
2. In a bowl add the rest of ingredients and toss to combine
3. Add fried zucchini and mix well

4. Pour over tahini dressing, mix well and serve

# RUTABAGA HASH

Serves:        **2**

Prep Time:   **10**   Minutes

Cook Time:   **20**   Minutes

Total Time:  **30**   Minutes

## INGREDIENTS

- 2 tablespoons olive oil
- 1 rutabaga
- ¼ cup onion
- ¼ cup red pepper
- 1 tsp salt
- ¼ tsp black pepper

## DIRECTIONS

1. In a skillet heat olive oil and fry rutabaga for 3-4 minutes
2. Cook for another 5-6 minutes or until rutabaga is tender
3. Add onion, red pepper, black pepper, salt and stir to combine
4. Garnish with dill and serve

# VEGAN CURRY

Serves: **4**

Prep Time: **10** Minutes

Cook Time: **20** Minutes

Total Time: **30** Minutes

## INGREDIENTS

- 1 tablespoon olive oil
- ¼ cup onion
- 2 stalks celery
- 1 garlic clove
- ¼ tsp coriander
- ¼ tsp cumin
- ¼ tsp turmeric
- ¼ tsp red pepper flakes
- 1 cauliflower
- 1 zucchini
- 2 tomatoes
- 1 tsp salt
- 1 cup vegetable broth
- 1 handful of baby spinach
- 1 tablespoon almonds
- 1 tablespoon cilantro

## DIRECTIONS

1. In a skillet heat olive oil and sauté celery, garlic and onions for 4-5 minutes or until vegetables are tender

2. Add cumin, spices, coriander, cumin, turmeric red pepper flakes stir to combine and cook for another 1-2 minutes

3. Add zucchini, cauliflower, tomatoes, broth, spinach, water and simmer on low heat for 15-20 minutes

4. Add remaining ingredients and simmer for another 4-5 minutes

5. Garnish curry and serve

# CAULIFLOWER WITH ROSEMARY

Serves:      **2**
Prep Time:   **5**   Minutes

Cook Time:   **15**   Minutes

Total Time:  **20**   Minutes

## INGREDIENTS

- 1 cauliflower
- 1 tablespoon rosemary
- 1 cup vegetable stock
- 2 garlic cloves
- salt

## DIRECTIONS

1. In a saucepan add cauliflower, stock and bring to a boil for 12-15 minutes
2. Blend cauliflower until smooth, add garlic, salt, rosemary and blend again
3. When ready pour in a bowl and serve

# BRUSSELS SPROUTS

Serves:         2
Prep Time:   **10**   Minutes

Cook Time:   **20**   Minutes

Total Time:   **30**   Minutes

## INGREDIENTS

- 1 tablespoon olive oil
- 2 shallots
- 2 cloves garlic
- 1 lb. brussels sprouts
- 1 cup vegetable stock
- 4 springs thyme
- ¼ cup pine nuts

## DIRECTIONS

1. In a pan heat olive oil and cook shallots until tender
2. Add garlic, sprouts, thyme, stock and cook for another 4-5 minutes
3. Cover and cook for another 10-12 minutes or until sprouts are soft
4. When ready add pine nuts and serve

# BREAD STUFFING

Serves:       **4**
Prep Time:    **10**   Minutes

Cook Time:    **25**   Minutes

Total Time:   **35**   Minutes

## INGREDIENTS

- One loaf candida diet bread
- 1 tablespoon olive oil
- ¼ cup celery
- ¼ cup onion
- ¼ cup mushrooms
- ¼ cup leeks
- 1 tsp thyme
- ¼ tsp salt
- 1 cup vegetable broth

## DIRECTIONS

1. Cut a loaf of candida diet bread cubes and place cubes aside
2. In a skillet heat olive oil add onion, celery, mushrooms and sauté for 5-10 minutes
3. Season with thyme, pepper, salt and stir to combine
4. Add vegetable mixture, broth, bread cubes and stir to combine

5. Place stuffing mixture into a casserole dish and bake for 12-15 minutes

6. Bake until golden brown and serve

# MOROCCAN STIR FRY

Serves:        **2**
Prep Time:   **10**   Minutes

Cook Time:   **20**   Minutes

Total Time:   **30**   Minutes

## INGREDIENTS

- ¼ cup onion
- 1 clove garlic
- 1 lb. ground turkey
- 1 tsp all spice
- 1 tsp cumin
- 1 tsp salt
- 2 cups cabbage
- 1 tablespoon mint
- 1 red bell pepper
- Zest of 1 lemon
- 1 tablespoon lemon juice
- plain yogurt
- pint leaves

## DIRECTIONS

1. In a skillet heat olive oil and sauté garlic, onion until soft

2. Add cumin, pepper, salt, all spice, ground turkey and sauté for 8-10 minutes

3. Add cabbage, red bell pepper, pint leaves, lemon zest and sauté for 4-5 minutes

4. When ready garnish with mint leaves, yogurt and serve

Serves:     **2**
Prep Time:  **10**  Minutes

Cook Time:  **30**  Minutes

Total Time:  **40**  Minutes

## INGREDIENTS

- 2 tablespoons olive oil
- 1 lb. cauliflower florets
- 1 tsp apple cider vinegar
- 1 tsp paprika
- ¼ tsp salt
- ¼ tsp onion powder
- ¼ tsp garlic powder
- 1 stalk celery
- 1 scallion
- 1 tablespoon parsley
- ranch dressing

## DIRECTIONS

1. In a bowl add salt, onion powder, garlic powder, paprika, apple cider vinegar, olive oil and whisk to combine
2. Add cauliflower florets to the bowl and toss to coat

3. Place florets on a prepared baking sheet and bake at 375 F for 25-30 minutes

4. When ready remove from the oven and transfer to a place

5. Garnish with scallion, celery, parsley, drizzle ranch dressing and serve

Serves:          **8-12**

Prep Time:       **10**   Minutes

Cook Time:       **20**   Minutes

Total Time:      **30**   Minutes

### INGREDIENTS

- 2 lb. steak
- 8-10 skewers
- Romain lettuce leaves
- Green onions

### MARINADE

- ¼ cup coconut aminos
- 1 tablespoon water
- 1 tablespoon olive oil
- 2 cloves garlic
- 2 cloves onions
- 1 tablespoon sesame seeds
- 1 tsp pepper flakes

### DIRECTIONS

1. Place all ingredients for the marinade in a bowl and mix well
2. Place steak cubes into the marinade bowl and let the meat marinade at least 8 hours

3. Preheat grill and place the steak kebabs on the grill

4. Cook for 4-5 minutes per side

5. When ready remove the kebabs from the gill and serve on lettuce leaves with green onions

## IRISH STEW

Serves:        **4**

Prep Time:    **15**   Minutes

Cook Time:   **45**   Minutes

Total Time:   **60**   Minutes

### INGREDIENTS

- 4-5 slices bacon
- 2 lb. beef
- ¼ cup flour
- ½ tsp black pepper
- 4 carrots
- ½ cup beef broth

### DIRECTIONS

1. Chop all ingredients in big chunks
2. In a large pot heat olive oil and add ingredients one by one
3. Cook for 5-6 or until slightly brown
4. Add remaining ingredients and cook until tender, 35-45 minutes
5. Season while stirring on low heat
6. When ready remove from heat and serve

# CHICKPEA STEW

Serves: **4**

Prep Time: **15** Minutes

Cook Time: **45** Minutes

Total Time: **60** Minutes

## INGREDIENTS

- 2 garlic cloves
- 1 tablespoon olive oil
- 2 scallions
- 1 red bell pepper
- 1 tsp paprika
- 1 tsp cumin
- 3 cups chickpeas
- 3-4 mint leaves
- ½ cup white wine

## DIRECTIONS

1. Chop all ingredients in big chunks
2. In a large pot heat olive oil and add ingredients one by one
3. Cook for 5-6 or until slightly brown
4. Add remaining ingredients and cook until tender, 35-45 minutes
5. Season while stirring on low heat

6. When ready remove from heat and serve

# CASSEROLE RECIPES

## BACON CASSEROLE

| | |
|---|---|
| Serves: | **4** |
| Prep Time: | **10** Minutes |
| Cook Time: | **15** Minutes |
| Total Time: | **25** Minutes |

### INGREDIENTS

- 4-5 slices bacon
- 3-4 tablespoons butter
- 5-6 tablespoons flour
- 2 cups milk
- 3 cups cheddar cheese
- 2 cups chicken breast
- 1 tsp seasoning mix

### DIRECTIONS

1. Sauté the veggies and set aside
2. Preheat the oven to 425 F
3. Transfer the sautéed veggies to a baking dish, add remaining ingredients to the baking dish
4. Mix well, add seasoning and place the dish in the oven
5. Bake for 12-15 minutes or until slightly brown

57

6. When ready remove from the oven and serve

ENCHILADA CASSEROLE

Serves:       **4**
Prep Time:    **10**  Minutes

Cook Time:    **25**  Minutes

Total Time:   **35**  Minutes

## INGREDIENTS

- 1 tablespoon olive oil
- 1 red onion
- 1 bell pepper
- 2 cloves garlic
- 1 can black beans
- 1 cup chicken
- 1 can green chilis
- 1 can enchilada sauce
- 1 cup cheddar cheese
- 1 cup sour cream

## DIRECTIONS

1. Sauté the veggies and set aside
2. Preheat the oven to 425 F
3. Transfer the sautéed veggies to a baking dish, add remaining ingredients to the baking dish
4. Mix well, add seasoning and place the dish in the oven

59

5.  Bake for 15-25 minutes or until slightly brown
6.  When ready remove from the oven and serve

## MEXICAN PIZZA

Serves:        **4**

Prep Time:   **10**   Minutes

Cook Time:   **20**   Minutes

Total Time:   **30**   Minutes

### INGREDIENTS
**Pizza**
- 1 ½ tsp cumin
- ½ tsp cayenne pepper
- 2 15-ounce cans black beans
- 8 corn tortillas
- 1 15-ounces can olives
- 3 tsp paprika
- 1 bell pepper
- 1 bunch green onions
- 1 cup cheese
- 1 red onion
- 4 tomatoes

### DIRECTIONS

1. Preheat the oven to 400F.
2. Bake the tortillas until crispy.

3. Heat the black beans, cumin, paprika, and cayenne until smooth.
4. Divide the bean among the tortillas, then spread evenly.
5. Top with the onion, bell pepper, olives and tomatoes.
6. Sprinkle the cheese on top.
7. Bake for 10 minutes.

Serves:        **4**
Prep Time:   **10**   Minutes

Cook Time:   **20**   Minutes

Total Time:   **30**   Minutes

## INGREDIENTS

- 1 ½ tbs basil
- 1 cup pizza sauce
- 6 chicken strips
- 1 10-ounces garlic bread
- 1 ½ cup cheese

## DIRECTIONS

1. Preheat the oven to 400F.
2. Place the garlic bread on a baking sheet.
3. Bake for 10 minutes, then spread the sauce over.
4. Cut the chicken strips and arrange over.
5. Sprinkle with cheese and basil.
6. Bake until the cheese melts.

Serves:        *6-8*
Prep Time:     *10*    Minutes

Cook Time:     *15*    Minutes

Total Time:    *25*    Minutes

## INGREDIENTS

- 1 pizza crust
- ½ cup tomato sauce
- ¼ black pepper
- 1 cup zucchini slices
- 1 cup mozzarella cheese
- 1 cup olives

## DIRECTIONS

1. Spread tomato sauce on the pizza crust
2. Place all the toppings on the pizza crust
3. Bake the pizza at 425 F for 12-15 minutes
4. When ready remove pizza from the oven and serve

# ZUCCHINI PIZZA

Serves:        **6**

Prep Time:    **25**   Minutes

Cook Time:    **15**   Minutes

Total Time:   **40**   Minutes

## INGREDIENTS

- 20 slices pepperoni
- 2 tsp herb seasoning
- 4 zucchinis
- 1 ½ tsp salt
- 1 lb mozzarella

## DIRECTIONS

1. Preheat the broiler.
2. Wash the zucchinis and cut off the ends.
3. Cut into even slices.
4. Spray a baking dish with non-stick spray.
5. Place the zucchini slices on the baking sheet.
6. Sprinkle with the salt and the herbs.
7. Cover with the grated cheese.
8. Broil until the cheese is starting to melt.
9. Place the pepperoni slices on top.
10. Broil for another 5 minutes, remove and serve

# SECOND COOKBOOK

## OLIVE GARDEN ZUPPA TOSCANA

Serves:        *6*
Prep Time:   *10*  Minutes

Cook Time:   *20*  Minutes

Total Time:   *30*  Minutes

### INGREDIENTS

- 4 turnips
- 3 kale leaves
- 1 onion
- 3 cloves garlic
- ½ bacon slices
- 1,5 L chicken broth
- 250 ml heavy cream
- 1 tsp salt
- 4 tablespoon parmesan
- 1 serving homemade Italian sausage

### DIRECTIONS

1. In a pot cook the bacon and transfer bacon aside
2. In the same pot add sausage and cook for 4-5 minutes
3. Add onion, chicken broth, turnings and cook until tender

4. Add kale, heavy cream, salt and stir
5. Add sausage back sprinkle with parmesan and serve

Serves:        *8*
Prep Time:   *10*   Minutes

Cook Time:   *30*   Minutes

Total Time:   *40*   Minutes

## INGREDIENTS

-   2 hot dog sausages

## CORN DOG BATTER

-   2 tablespoons almond flour
-   ½ tsp xanthan gum
-   ½ tsp salt
-   ½ tsp baking soda
-   ¼ tsp baking powder
-   ½ tsp garlic powder
-   1 egg
-   1 tablespoon water

## DIRECTIONS

1.  In a bowl add all ingredients for the corn dogs and whisk together
2.  Dip one sausage at a time and roll the skewer
3.  Add the corn dog into hot oil and fry for 30 seconds
4.  Serve when ready

Serves:        **6**

Prep Time:    **10**   Minutes

Cook Time:    **50**   Minutes

Total Time:    **60**   Minutes

## INGREDIENTS

- ½ onion
- ¼ lb. cabbage
- 3 cloves garlic
- 1 tablespoon olive oil
- ¾ lb. ground chicken
- 1.5 lb. ground pork
- 2 tablespoons parsley
- 1 tsp salt
- 1 tsp black pepper
- 1 tsp mustard
- 1 tablespoon Worcestershire sauce
- 3 boiled eggs

## DIRECTIONS

1. Preheat oven to 325 F
2. In a frying pan mix all the veggies cook until soft

3. In a bowl mix ground meat, cooked veggies, parsley and spices
4. Add half the meatloaf mixture to a loaf pan and top with boiled eggs
5. Bake for 40-45 minutes, remove and serve

# THAI CHICKEN WINGS

Serves:         **5**
Prep Time:    **10**   Minutes

Cook Time:    **50**   Minutes

Total Time:    **60**   Minutes

## INGREDIENTS

- 2 lb. chicken drumsticks
- 1 lb. chicken wings
- 1 tablespoon olive oil
- 1 tsp salt
- 1 tsp black pepper
- 4 tablespoons thai sweet chili sauce

## DIRECTIONS

1. Preheat the oven to 350 F
2. Add the drumsticks and wings to a baking pan and drizzle the olive oil
3. Sprinkle with salt and pepper all over the wings
4. Bake for 40-45 minutes
5. Remove from the oven and transfer to a frying pan, add thai sweet chili sauce

# CHICKEN STIR-FRY

Serves:        *6*
Prep Time:    *10*  Minutes

Cook Time:    *20*  Minutes

Total Time:   *30*  Minutes

## INGREDIENTS

- 5 chicken breasts
- 2 onions
- 2 bell peppers
- 1 cup broccoli florets
- 1 carrot
- 1 clove garlic
- salt
- 1 tablespoon canola oil
- 2 cups brown rice

## DIRECTIONS

1. While rice is cooking, sauté chicken the chicken and set aside
2. Sauté onions, garlic, bell pepper, add carrots and broccoli
3. Add chicken back to skillet, season with salt and pepper
4. Serve with brown rice topped with the chicken mixture

# HUMMUS

Serves: **4**
Prep Time: **10** Minutes

Cook Time: **20** Minutes

Total Time: **30** Minutes

### INGREDIENTS

- 1 can chickpeas
- 1/3 cup water
- 2 tablespoons tahini
- 1 clove garlic
- ½ tsp salt
- 1 tablespoon oil
- 1 tablespoon lemon juice

### DIRECTIONS

1. Place all ingredients in a blender and blend until smooth
2. Pour hummus into a container and serve

# GRILLED SALMON WITH BASIL

Serves:        **4**

Prep Time:   **10**   Minutes

Cook Time:   **20**   Minutes

Total Time:   **30**   Minutes

## INGREDIENTS

- 3 salmon steaks
- 2 tablespoons lemon juice
- 2 tablespoons olive oil
- 1 tablespoon basil
- 3 lemon wedges

## DIRECTIONS

1. In a bowl mix basil, olive oil, lemon juice and brush both sides of salmon
2. Grill for 10-12 minutes at 150 F
3. Serve with lemon wedges

# TUNA MELT

Serves:        **2**
Prep Time:   **10**   Minutes

Cook Time:   **10**   Minutes

Total Time:  **20**   Minutes

## INGREDIENTS

- 1 can tuna
- 1 whole wheat English muffins
- ½ cup canola mayonnaise
- 3 tomato slices
- 1 tablespoon sweet pickle
- 3 slices cheddar cheese
- ½ tablespoon mustard
- 1 tsp tabasco sauce

## DIRECTIONS

1. In a bowl mix sweet pickle, tuna, mayonnaise, mustard and tabasco sauce and mix well
2. Spread tuna mixture on each English muffin
3. Top with tomato and cheddar cheese
4. Broil 4-5 minutes until cheese melts

Serves:        *2*
Prep Time:    *10*  Minutes

Cook Time:   *10*  Minutes

Total Time:   *20*  Minutes

## INGREDIENTS

- 2 whole wheat pita bread rounds
- 2 tomatoes
- 3 tablespoons olive oil
- 3-pieces mozzarella cheese
- 1 garlic clove
- 1 cup basil leaves
- salt

## DIRECTIONS

1. Add mozzarella, garlic, basil, tomato and tomato in a bowl and sprinkle with salt, pepper and drizzle with olive oil
2. Place all ingredients in warmed pita pockets

# SCRAMBLED EGG SANDWICH

Serves:           **2**
Prep Time:    **10**   Minutes

Cook Time:    **10**   Minutes

Total Time:    **20**   Minutes

## INGREDIENTS

- 3 slices whole grain bread
- 1 tsp butter
- 1 cloves garlic
- 1 tablespoon dried parsley
- 1 cup egg substitute
- 1 tomato
- ½ tsp salt
- ¼ tsp pepper
- 10 basil leaves
- ½ cup cheddar cheese

## DIRECTIONS

1. In a pan melt butter, add garlic, eggs and cook for 2-3 minutes
2. Arrange the egg mixture onto 4 slices of toasted bread
3. Top with basil leaves and sprinkle with cheese

# GREEK PIZZA

| | | |
|---|---|---|
| Serves: | **6-8** | |
| Prep Time: | **10** | Minutes |
| Cook Time: | **15** | Minutes |
| Total Time: | **25** | Minutes |

## INGREDIENTS

- 1 pizza crust
- 1 tablespoon olive oil
- 6 oz. spinach
- ¼ cup basil
- 1 tsp oregano
- 1 cup mozzarella cheese
- 1 tomato
- ½ cup feta cheese

## DIRECTIONS

1. Spread tomato sauce on the pizza crust
2. Place all the toppings on the pizza crust
3. Bake the pizza at 425 F for 12-15 minutes
4. When ready remove pizza from the oven and serve

Serves:        *6-8*
Prep Time:     *10*  Minutes

Cook Time:     *15*  Minutes

Total Time:    *25*  Minutes

## INGREDIENTS

- 1 cup cooked chicken breast
- ½ cup bbq sauce
- 1 pizza crust
- 1 tablespoon olive oil
- 1 cup cheese
- 1 cup tomatoes

## DIRECTIONS

1. Spread tomato sauce on the pizza crust
2. Place all the toppings on the pizza crust
3. Bake the pizza at 425 F for 12-15 minutes
4. When ready remove pizza from the oven and serve

# MARGHERITA PIZZA

Serves:        **6-8**

Prep Time:   **10**   Minutes

Cook Time:   **15**   Minutes

Total Time:   **25**   Minutes

## INGREDIENTS

- 1 pizza crust
- 1 tablespoon garlic
- 1 tsp salt
- 2-3 tomatoes
- 1 pizza crust
- 4 oz. mozzarella cheese
- 6-8 basil leaves
- ¼ cup parmesan cheese
- ¼ cup feta cheese

## DIRECTIONS

1. Spread tomato sauce on the pizza crust
2. Place all the toppings on the pizza crust
3. Bake the pizza at 425 F for 12-15 minutes
4. When ready remove pizza from the oven and serve

# EDAMAME FRITATTA

Serves:        **2**

Prep Time:   **10**   Minutes

Cook Time:  **20**   Minutes

Total Time:  **30**   Minutes

## INGREDIENTS

- 1 cup edamame
- 1 tablespoon olive oil
- ½ red onion
- 2 eggs
- ¼ tsp salt
- 2 oz. cheddar cheese
- 1 garlic clove
- ¼ tsp dill

## DIRECTIONS

1. In a bowl whisk eggs with salt and cheese
2. In a frying pan heat olive oil and pour egg mixture
3. Add remaining ingredients and mix well
4. Serve when ready

# PICADILLO

Serves: **3**

Prep Time: **10** Minutes

Cook Time: **30** Minutes

Total Time: **40** Minutes

## INGREDIENTS
**Sofrito**
- 2 tbs olive oil
- 5 oz red bell pepper
- 1 oz garlic
- 7 oz onion

**Picadillo**
- 5 oz potatoes
- 1 oz raisins
- 1 ½ tsp oregano
- 1/3 cup white wine
- 1 tbs tomato paste
- 1 lb beef
- 7 oz tomatoes
- 2 tsp cumin
- 1 tsp cinnamon
- 1 tsp salt
- 3 oz olives
- 2 tbs olive brine

- 2 bay leaves

## DIRECTIONS

1. Sauté the pepper, onions and garlic in oil until tender
2. Add the oregano, cinnamon, bay leaves and cumin and sauté a little bit more
3. Add in the beef, tomato paste, wine, potatoes, tomatoes, raisins, and salt
4. Simmer for about 15 minutes partially covered
5. Add in the olives and let picadillo cook for about 10 minutes
6. Stir in the olive brine when finished
7. Season and serve

Serves:       **2**
Prep Time:    **10**   minutes

Cook Time:    **30**   minutes

Total Time:   **40**   Minutes

## INGREDIENTS

- **1/3 cup lime juice**
- **1 onion**
- **1 ½ cup white wine**
- **1/3 cup raisins**
- **½ cup oil**
- **1 bell pepper**
- **1 ½ cup peas**
- **1/3 cup orange juice**
- **1 lb potatoes**
- **¾ cup alcaparrado**
- **4 cloves garlic**
- **1 can tomato sauce**
- **Salt**
- **Pepper**
- **1 chicken**

## DIRECTIONS

1. Mix lime juice, orange juice, chicken, garlic, salt, and pepper

2. Chill for at least 1 hour

3. Cook the marinated chicken for about 10 minutes until browned

4. Cook the pepper and onion until soft, then add wine and cook for another 5 minutes

5. Return the chicken to pan along with the remaining marinade, alcaparrado, tomato sauce, potatoes, ½ cup water, raisins, salt, and pepper.

6. Bring to a boil, then reduce the heat and cook for about 45 minutes

7. Stir in the peas and serve

# CHICKEN AND RICE

Serves:        **6**

Prep Time:    **10**   minutes

Cook Time:   **50**   minutes

Total Time:   **60**   Minutes

## INGREDIENTS

- 3 cloves garlic
- 12 oz diced tomatoes
- 2 tsp cumin
- 3 tsp red pepper flakes
- 4 tbs oil
- 4 cups chicken broth
- 1 tsp saffron
- 3 bay leaves
- 1 tsp salt
- 1/3 tsp black pepper
- 2 ½ lbs chicken
- 2 cups brown rice
- 1 red onion
- 3 bell peppers
- 1 ½ cups green olives
- 3 tbs lime juice

## DIRECTIONS

1. Mix the red pepper flakes, lime juice, garlic, salt and pepper
2. Add the chicken and toss to coat
3. Allow to marinate overnight
4. Cook on both sides until golden
5. Warm up the broth and stir in the saffron
6. Saute the onions and peppers until soft.
7. Add in the tomatoes, bay leaves, cumin and rice
8. Cook for about 5 minutes until the juices are absorbed
9. Pour in the broth, add the chicken on top and bring to a boil
10. Reduce the heat and cook covered on low for about 35 minutes
11. Cook uncovered for another 15 minutes
12. Serve topped with cilantro

# LOBSTER CREOLE

Serves:        *10*
Prep Time:     *20*   minutes

Cook Time:     *40*   minutes

Total Time:    *60*   Minutes

## INGREDIENTS

- 6 lobster tails
- 15 oz can crush tomatoes
- 2 lb shrimp
- 1/3 cup olive oil
- 2 onions
- 1 bunch Italian parley
- 1 bay leaf
- 1 cup ketchup
- 2 tsp tabasco
- 1 red pepper
- 5 garlic cloves
- 1 can pimentos
- 2 tbs Worcestershire sauce
- 5 oz tomato sauce
- 1/3 cup wine
- 2 tbs vinegar

-   Salt
-   Pepper

## DIRECTIONS

1.  Cut lobster tails into rings and sauté in hot oil until the shells turn red
2.  Sauté the onion, garlic, red pepper and bay leaf in the remaining oil for about 10 minutes
3.  Stir in the Worcestershire sauce, tomato paste, wine, vinegar, parsley, crushed tomatoes, ketchup, and pimentos
4.  Bring to a simmer and cook for 15 minutes, then season with salt and pepper
5.  Return the lobster to the pot and simmer for at least 15 minutes
6.  Stir in hot sauce
7.  Serve immediately

# MOROS CUBAN

Serves: **8**

Prep Time: **10** minutes

Cook Time: **60** minutes

Total Time: **70** Minutes

## INGREDIENTS

- 2 cups rice
- 2 tsp cumin
- 2 tsp fennel
- 1 lb black beans
- 5 cups water
- 1 lb ham
- 3 oregano sprigs
- 3 cloves garlic
- 3 tbs tomato paste
- 1 jalapeno chile
- 3 tbs olive oil
- 2 cups onion
- 2 cups green bell pepper
- 2 ½ tsp salt
- ½ tsp pepper
- 3 bay leaves

## DIRECTIONS

1. Rinse the rice and the beans under cold water
2. Place the beans, ham, bay leaves, oregano sprigs, jalapeno and water in a stockpot
3. Bring to a boil, then reduce the heat and simmer for about 40 minutes
4. Pour bean mixture into a colander placed into a bowl, reserving 4 cups liquid
5. Discard jalapenos halves, oregano and bay leaves
6. Remove the ham hock and chop the meat
7. Cook the onion and pepper in hot oil until soft
8. Stir in the cumin, fennel, tomato paste and cook for 5 minutes
9. Add the rice and cook 1 more minute
10. Add ham, black beans, salt, pepper and black beans liquid and bring to a boil
11. Reduce the heat and simmer for 20 minutes
12. Serve immediately

# CAULIFLOWER BOWL

Serves:        **4**

Prep Time:     **10**   minutes

Cook Time:     **10**   minutes

Total Time:    **20**   Minutes

## INGREDIENTS

- 1 sweet potato
- 1 tsp cumin
- 1 tsp oregano
- 4 cloves garlic
- 3 tbs lime juice
- 1/3 cup cilantro
- 5 cups cauliflower florets
- 3 tsp olive oil
- 15 oz black beans
- 1 avocado
- ½ cup pico de gallo
- 3 tsp salt
- 1 tsp black pepper
- 1/3 cup orange juice

## DIRECTIONS

1. Mix salt, oil and pepper in a bowl
2. Toss the sweet potatoes in the mixture
3. Roast for at least 10 minutes until tender
4. Mix the lime juice, orange juice, 1 minced garlic clove, 1/3 cup cilantro, oregano, salt, and cumin in a bowl
5. Pulse the cauliflower using a food processor
6. Cook the remaining garlic in hot oil for about half a minute
7. Add the cauliflower, salt, pepper and cook for about 5 minutes
8. Remove from heat and stir in the cilantro
9. Divide among bowls and serve topped with sweet potato, avocado, black beans and pico de gallo

# CHICKEN WITH SALSA

Serves:        **4**
Prep Time:     **15**  Minutes

Cook Time:     **15**  Minutes

Total Time:    **30**  Minutes

**INGREDIENTS**
Chicken:
- Pinch chilli flakes
- 1 lb chicken breasts
- 3 tsp garlic granules
- 5 oz grapefruit juice
- 3 tsp cumin
- 2 tsp paprika
- 3 tbs olive oil

Salsa:
- 5 oz grapefruit segments
- 1/3 red onion
- 3 tbs olive oil
- 1 ½ tbs jalapeno pepper
- 3 tbs grapefruit juice
- 2 tbs coriander leaf
- 4 oz jicama

## DIRECTIONS

1.  Mix the chicken ingredients together except for the chicken breast
2.  Place the chicken into the mixture and allow o marinate covered for at least 1 hour
3.  Mix the salsa ingredients together in a bowl
4.  Cover and refrigerate
5.  Grill the chicken for about 5 minutes per side until done
6.  Serve with salsa

# MEXICAN CHICKEN

Serves:          **4**

Prep Time:    **10**   Minutes

Cook Time:    **20**   Minutes

Total Time:    **30**   Minutes

## INGREDIENTS

- 2 tsp oil
- 2 chicken breasts
- 2 bell peppers
- 2 cups broccoli florets
- 1 ½ tsp cumin
- 1 tsp cayenne pepper
- 1 tsp paprika

## DIRECTIONS

1. Heat a pan
2. Heat the oil for about 20 seconds
3. Add diced chicken and cook for 5 minutes
4. Add the broccoli and peppers and cook for another 10 minutes
5. Add the spices
6. Cook until the water is absorbed

# GRILLED SALMON

Serves:        *4*
Prep Time:     *5*    Minutes

Cook Time:     *10*   Minutes

Total Time:    *15*   Minutes

## INGREDIENTS

- 2 limes juiced
- 1 tbs cilantro
- 1 ½ tsp cumin
- 1 ½ tsp paprika
- 2 lbs salmon
- 1 ½ tbs oil
- 1 tsp onion powder
- 1 tsp chili powder
- 1 avocado
- 2 tsp salt
- 1 red onion

## DIRECTIONS

1. Mix the chili powder, onion powder, cumin, paprika, salt and pepper together
2. Rub the salmon with the mix and oil
3. Refrigerate for 30 minutes

4. Preheat the grill
5. Mix the avocado with lime juice, cilantro, and onion together
6. Grill the salmon
7. Serve topped with the avocado salsa

# CUBAN QUINOA

Serves:        **8**

Prep Time:     **15**   Minutes

Cook Time:     **4**    Hours

Total Time:    **4h 15**   Minutes

## INGREDIENTS

- 1 jalapeno
- 2 cups enchilada sauce
- 1 ½ cup chicken broth
- 1 can black beans
- 2 lb butternut squash
- 1 cup corn
- 1 cup quinoa
- 1 tsp garlic
- 1 can tomatoes

## DIRECTIONS

1. Peel and deseed the butternut squash
2. Cut into cubes, then place in the slow cooker
3. Add the corn, quinoa, garlic, tomatoes, black beans, jalapeno, enchilada sauce and the chicken broth
4. Give it a good stir, then cook for 4 hours
5. Allow the liquid to absorb while on low for 30 minutes
6. Season with salt and pepper

ROASTED SQUASH

| | | |
|---|---|---|
| Serves: | **3-4** | |
| Prep Time: | **10** | Minutes |
| Cook Time: | **20** | Minutes |
| Total Time: | **30** | Minutes |

**INGREDIENTS**

- 2 delicata squashes
- 2 tablespoons olive oil
- 1 tsp curry powder
- 1 tsp salt

**DIRECTIONS**

1. Preheat the oven to 400 F
2. Cut everything in half lengthwise
3. Toss everything with olive oil and place onto a prepared baking sheet
4. Roast for 18-20 minutes at 400 F or until golden brown
5. When ready remove from the oven and serve

Serves:          *2*
Prep Time:    *10*   Minutes

Cook Time:   *20*   Minutes

Total Time:   *30*   Minutes

## INGREDIENTS

- 1 lb. brussels sprouts
- 1 tablespoon olive oil
- 1 tablespoon parmesan cheese
- 1 tsp garlic powder
- 1 tsp seasoning

## DIRECTIONS

1. Preheat the oven to 425 F
2. In a bowl toss everything with olive oil and seasoning
3. Spread everything onto a prepared baking sheet
4. Bake for 8-10 minutes or until crisp
5. When ready remove from the oven and serve

# ZUCCHINI CHIPS

Serves:       **2**

Prep Time:  **10**  Minutes

Cook Time:  **20**  Minutes

Total Time:  **30**  Minutes

## INGREDIENTS

- 1 lb. zucchini
- 1 tablespoon olive oil
- 1 tablespoon parmesan cheese
- 1 tsp garlic powder
- 1 tsp seasoning

## DIRECTIONS

1. Preheat the oven to 425 F
2. In a bowl toss everything with olive oil and seasoning
3. Spread everything onto a prepared baking sheet
4. Bake for 8-10 minutes or until crisp
5. When ready remove from the oven and serve

Serves:          **2**
Prep Time:    **10**  Minutes

Cook Time:    **20**  Minutes

Total Time:   **30**  Minutes

## INGREDIENTS

- 1 lb. carrot
- 1 tablespoon olive oil
- 1 tablespoon parmesan cheese
- 1 tsp garlic powder
- 1 tsp seasoning

## DIRECTIONS

1. Preheat the oven to 425 F
2. In a bowl toss everything with olive oil and seasoning
3. Spread everything onto a prepared baking sheet
4. Bake for 8-10 minutes or until crisp
5. When ready remove from the oven and serve

# *PASTA*

## SIMPLE SPAGHETTI

Serves:          **2**
Prep Time:     **5**   Minutes

Cook Time:    **15**   Minutes

Total Time:   **20**   Minutes

### INGREDIENTS

- 10 oz. spaghetti
- 2 eggs
- ½ cup parmesan cheese
- 1 tsp black pepper
- Olive oil
- 1 tsp parsley
- 2 cloves garlic

### DIRECTIONS

1. In a pot boil spaghetti (or any other type of pasta), drain and set aside
2. In a bowl whish eggs with parmesan cheese
3. In a skillet heat olive oil, add garlic and cook for 1-2 minutes
4. Pour egg mixture and mix well
5. Add pasta and stir well

6. When ready garnish with parsley and serve

# CORN PASTA

Serves:      **2**

Prep Time:   **5**   Minutes

Cook Time:  **15**  Minutes

Total Time:  **20**  Minutes

## INGREDIENTS

- 1 lb. pasta
- 4 oz. cheese
- ¼ sour cream
- 1 onion
- 2 cloves garlic
- 1 tsp cumin
- 2 cups corn kernels
- 1 tsp chili powder
- 1 tablespoon cilantro

## DIRECTIONS

1. In a pot boil spaghetti (or any other type of pasta), drain and set aside
2. Place all the ingredients for the sauce in a pot and bring to a simmer
3. Add pasta and mix well
4. When ready garnish with parmesan cheese and serve

# ARTICHOKE PASTA

Serves:        2

Prep Time:     5    Minutes

Cook Time:     15   Minutes

Total Time:    20   Minutes

## INGREDIENTS

- ¼ cup olive oil
- 1 jar artichokes
- 2 cloves garlic
- 1 tablespoon thyme leaves
- 1 lb. pasta
- 2 tablespoons butter
- 1. Cup basil
- ½ cup parmesan cheese

## DIRECTIONS

1. In a pot boil spaghetti (or any other type of pasta), drain and set aside
2. Place all the ingredients for the sauce in a pot and bring to a simmer
3. Add pasta and mix well
4. When ready garnish with parmesan cheese and serve

# SALAD

## SLAW

Serves:        *1*
Prep Time:    5    Minutes

Cook Time:    5    Minutes

Total Time:    *10*    Minutes

### INGREDIENTS

- 1 cabbage
- 1 bunch of baby carrots
- ½ cucumber
- 1 bun of cilantro
- 1 bunch of basil
- 1 onion

### DIRECTIONS

1. In a bowl combine all ingredients together and mix well
2. Serve with dressing

Serves: **1**
Prep Time: **5** Minutes

Cook Time: **5** Minutes

Total Time: **10** Minutes

## INGREDIENTS

- 1 egg
- ¼ cup rice vinegar
- 1 tablespoon coconut aminos
- 1 tablespoon sriracha
- 1 tablespoon maple syrup

## DIRECTIONS

1. In a bowl combine all ingredients together and mix well
2. Serve with dressing

Serves:      **1**

Prep Time:   **5**   Minutes

Cook Time:   **5**   Minutes

Total Time:   **10**   Minutes

## INGREDIENTS

- 2 cups arugula leaves
- ¼ cup cranberries
- ¼ cup honey
- ¼ cup pecans
- 1 cup salad dressing

## DIRECTIONS

1. In a bowl combine all ingredients together and mix well
2. Serve with dressing

# MASOOR SALAD

Serves: **1**

Prep Time: **5** Minutes

Cook Time: **5** Minutes

Total Time: **10** Minutes

## INGREDIENTS

- ¼ cup masoor
- ¼ cup cucumber
- ½ cup carrot
- ¼ cup tomatoes
- ¼ cup onion

## SALAD DRESSING

- ¼ tablespoon olive oil
- 1 tsp lemon juice
- ¼ tsp green chillies
- ½ tsp black pepper

## DIRECTIONS

1. In a bowl combine all ingredients together and mix well
2. Add salad dressing, toss well and serve

Serves:        *1*
Prep Time:   *5*   Minutes
Cook Time:   *5*   Minutes
Total Time:  *10*  Minutes

## INGREDIENTS

- 1 cup muskmelon
- ½ cup pear cubes
- ½ cup apple cubes
- Salad dressing

## DIRECTIONS

1. In a bowl combine all ingredients together and mix well
2. Add salad dressing, toss well and serve

# CITRUS WATERMELON SALAD

Serves: **1**

Prep Time: **5** Minutes

Cook Time: **5** Minutes

Total Time: **10** Minutes

## INGREDIENTS

- 2 cups watermelon
- ¼ cup orange
- ¼ cup sweet lime
- ¼ cup pomegranate

## SALAD DRESSING

- 1 tsp olive oil
- 1 tsp lemon juice
- 1 tablespoon parsley

## DIRECTIONS

1. In a bowl combine all ingredients together and mix well
2. Add salad dressing, toss well and serve

# POTATO SALAD

| | | |
|---|---|---|
| Serves: | **2** | |
| Prep Time: | **5** | Minutes |
| Cook Time: | **10** | Minutes |
| Total Time: | **15** | Minutes |

## INGREDIENTS

- 5 potatoes
- 1 tsp cumin seeds
- 1/3 cup oil
- 2 tsp mustard
- 1 red onion
- 2 cloves garlic
- 1/3 cup lemon juice
- 1 tsp sea salt

## DIRECTIONS

1. Steam the potatoes until tender
2. Mix mustard, turmeric powder, lemon juice, cumin seeds, and salt
3. Place the potatoes in a bowl and pour the lemon mixture over
4. Add the chopped onion and minced garlic over
5. Stir to coat and refrigerate covered
6. Add oil and stir before serving

# CARROT SALAD

Serves:        *2*
Prep Time:     *5*  Minutes
Cook Time:     *5*  Minutes
Total Time:    *10*  Minutes

## INGREDIENTS

- 1 ½ tbs lemon juice
- 1/3 tsp salt
- ¼ tsp black pepper
- 2 tbs olive oil
- 1/3 lb carrots
- 1 tsp mustard

## DIRECTIONS

1. Mix mustard, lemon juice and oil together
2. Peel and shred the carrots in a bowl
3. Stir in the dressing and season with salt and pepper
4. Mix well and allow to chill for at least 30 minutes

Serves:          **2**
Prep Time:    **5**   Minutes

Cook Time:    **5**   Minutes

Total Time:   **10**  Minutes

## INGREDIENTS

- 2 tbs lemon juice
- 1 tsp cumin
- 1 tsp paprika
- 3 tbs olive oil
- 2 cloves garlic
- 5 carrots
- Salt
- Pepper

## DIRECTIONS

1. Peel and slice the carrots
2. Add the carrots in boiled water and simmer for at least 5 minutes
3. Drain and rinse the carrots under cold water
4. Add in a bowl
5. Mix the lemon juice, garlic, cumin, paprika, and olive oil together

6. Pour the mixture over the carrots and toss then season with salt and pepper
7. Serve immediately

# AVOCADO CHICKEN SALAD

Serves:        2

Prep Time:    5    Minutes

Cook Time:    5    Minutes

Total Time:   *10*   Minutes

## INGREDIENTS

- 3 tsp lime juice
- 3 tbs cilantro
- 1 chicken breast
- 1 avocado
- 1/3 cup onion
- 1 apple
- 1 cup celery
- Salt
- Pepper
- Olive oil

## DIRECTIONS

1. Dice the chicken breast
2. Season with salt and pepper and cook into a greased skillet until golden
3. Dice the vegetables and place over the chicken in a bowl
4. Mash the avocado and sprinkle in the cilantro

5. Season with salt and pepper and add lime juice
6. Serve drizzled with olive oil

# THIRD COOKBOOK

## BEANS OMELETTE

Serves:        **1**
Prep Time:     **5**   Minutes

Cook Time:    **10**   Minutes

Total Time:   **15**   Minutes

### INGREDIENTS

- 2 eggs
- ¼ tsp salt
- ¼ tsp black pepper
- 1 tablespoon olive oil
- ¼ cup cheese
- ¼ tsp basil
- 1 cup beans

### DIRECTIONS

1. In a bowl combine all ingredients together and mix well
2. In a skillet heat olive oil and pour the egg mixture
3. Cook for 1-2 minutes per side
4. When ready remove omelette from the skillet and serve

| Serves: | 2 | |
|---|---|---|
| Prep Time: | 5 | Minutes |
| Cook Time: | 30 | Minutes |
| Total Time: | 35 | Minutes |

## INGREDIENTS

- 1 tsp vanilla extract
- 1 tablespoon honey
- 1 lb. rolled oats
- 2 tablespoons sesame seeds
- ¼ lb. almonds
- ¼ lb. berries

## DIRECTIONS

1. Preheat the oven to 325 F
2. Spread the granola onto a baking sheet
3. Bake for 12-15 minutes, remove and mix everything
4. Bake for another 12-15 minutes or until slightly brown
5. When ready remove from the oven and serve

# MANDARIN MUFFINS

Serves:        *8-12*
Prep Time:     *10*    Minutes
Cook Time:     *20*    Minutes
Total Time:    *30*    Minutes

## INGREDIENTS

- 2 eggs
- 1 tablespoon olive oil
- 1 cup milk
- 2 cups whole wheat flour
- 1 tsp baking soda
- ¼ tsp baking soda
- 1 tsp ginger
- 1 cup mandarin
- ¼ cup molasses

## DIRECTIONS

1. In a bowl combine all wet ingredients
2. In another bowl combine all dry ingredients
3. Combine wet and dry ingredients together
4. Pour mixture into 8-12 prepared muffin cups, fill 2/3 of the cups
5. Bake for 18-20 minutes at 375 F

# BANANA MUFFINS

| | |
|---|---|
| Serves: | *8-12* |
| Prep Time: | *10* Minutes |
| Cook Time: | *20* Minutes |
| Total Time: | *30* Minutes |

## INGREDIENTS

- 2 eggs
- 1 tablespoon olive oil
- 1 cup milk
- 2 cups whole wheat flour
- 1 tsp baking soda
- ¼ tsp baking soda
- 1 tsp cinnamon
- 1 cup mashed banana

## DIRECTIONS

1. In a bowl combine all wet ingredients
2. In another bowl combine all dry ingredients
3. Combine wet and dry ingredients together
4. Fold in mashed banana and mix well
5. Pour mixture into 8-12 prepared muffin cups, fill 2/3 of the cups
6. Bake for 18-20 minutes at 375 F

# POMEGRANATE MUFFINS

Serves:        *8-12*
Prep Time:     *10*   Minutes

Cook Time:     *20*   Minutes

Total Time:    *30*   Minutes

## INGREDIENTS

- 2 eggs
- 1 tablespoon olive oil
- 1 cup milk
- 2 cups whole wheat flour
- 1 tsp baking soda
- ¼ tsp baking soda
- 1 tsp cinnamon
- 1 cup pomegranate

## DIRECTIONS

1. In a bowl combine all wet ingredients
2. In another bowl combine all dry ingredients
3. Combine wet and dry ingredients together
4. Pour mixture into 8-12 prepared muffin cups, fill 2/3 of the cups
5. Bake for 18-20 minutes at 375 F
6. When ready remove from the oven and serve

# STRAWBERRY MUFFINS

Serves:         *8-12*
Prep Time:      *10*    Minutes

Cook Time:      *20*    Minutes

Total Time:     *30*    Minutes

## INGREDIENTS

- 2 eggs
- 1 tablespoon olive oil
- 1 cup milk
- 2 cups whole wheat flour
- 1 tsp baking soda
- ¼ tsp baking soda
- 1 tsp cinnamon
- 1 cup strawberries

## DIRECTIONS

1. In a bowl combine all wet ingredients
2. In another bowl combine all dry ingredients
3. Combine wet and dry ingredients together
4. Fold in strawberries and mix well
5. Pour mixture into 8-12 prepared muffin cups, fill 2/3 of the cups
6. Bake for 18-20 minutes at 375 F

# PLUMS MUFFINS

Serves:        **8-12**
Prep Time:     **10**    Minutes

Cook Time:     **20**    Minutes

Total Time:    **30**    Minutes

## INGREDIENTS

- 2 eggs
- 1 tablespoon olive oil
- 1 cup milk
- 2 cups whole wheat flour
- 1 tsp baking soda
- ¼ tsp baking soda
- 1 tsp cinnamon
- 1 cup plums

## DIRECTIONS

1. In a bowl combine all wet ingredients
2. In another bowl combine all dry ingredients
3. Combine wet and dry ingredients together
4. Pour mixture into 8-12 prepared muffin cups, fill 2/3 of the cups
5. Bake for 18-20 minutes at 375 F
6. When ready remove from the oven and serve

# ZUCCHINI OMELETTE

Serves:        *1*
Prep Time:    5    Minutes
Cook Time:   *10*  Minutes
Total Time:  *15*  Minutes

## INGREDIENTS

- 2 eggs
- ¼ tsp salt
- ¼ tsp black pepper
- 1 tablespoon olive oil
- ¼ cup cheese
- ¼ tsp basil
- 1 cup zucchini

## DIRECTIONS

1. In a bowl combine all ingredients together and mix well
2. In a skillet heat olive oil and pour the egg mixture
3. Cook for 1-2 minutes per side
4. When ready remove omelette from the skillet and serve

# BASIL OMELETTE

Serves:        **1**
Prep Time:     **5**     Minutes

Cook Time:     **10**    Minutes

Total Time:    **15**    Minutes

## INGREDIENTS

- 2 eggs
- ¼ tsp salt
- ¼ tsp black pepper
- 1 tablespoon olive oil
- ¼ cup cheese
- ¼ tsp basil
- 1 cup red onion

## DIRECTIONS

1. In a bowl combine all ingredients together and mix well
2. In a skillet heat olive oil and pour the egg mixture
3. Cook for 1-2 minutes per side
4. When ready remove omelette from the skillet and serve

# MUSHROOM OMELETTE

Serves:        *1*
Prep Time:   *5*   Minutes

Cook Time:   *10*   Minutes

Total Time:   *15*   Minutes

## INGREDIENTS

- 2 eggs
- ¼ tsp salt
- ¼ tsp black pepper
- 1 tablespoon olive oil
- ¼ cup cheese
- ¼ tsp basil
- 1 cup mushrooms

## DIRECTIONS

1. In a bowl combine all ingredients together and mix well
2. In a skillet heat olive oil and pour the egg mixture
3. Cook for 1-2 minutes per side
4. When ready remove omelette from the skillet and serve

# PUMPKIN OMELETTE

Serves:          *1*
Prep Time:    *5*    Minutes

Cook Time:   *10*   Minutes

Total Time:   *15*   Minutes

## INGREDIENTS

- 2 eggs
- ¼ tsp salt
- ¼ tsp black pepper
- 1 tablespoon olive oil
- ¼ cup cheese
- ¼ tsp basil
- 1 cup pumpkin puree

## DIRECTIONS

1. In a bowl combine all ingredients together and mix well
2. In a skillet heat olive oil and pour the egg mixture
3. Cook for 1-2 minutes per side
4. When ready remove omelette from the skillet and serve

# BLUEBERRIES OATMEAL

Serves:        **2**

Prep Time:     **10**   Minutes

Cook Time:     **8**    Hours

Total Time:    **8**    Hours

## INGREDIENTS

- 1/3 cup oats
- 1/3 cup blueberries
- 2 tbs maple syrup
- 1/3 cup coconut milk
- ½ tsp vanilla
- 1 banana
- 1 ½ tsp chia seeds

## DIRECTIONS

1. Mix the oats and chia seeds together
2. Pour in the milk and top with blueberries and sliced banana
3. Refrigerate for at least 8 hours
4. Stir in the maple syrup and serve

# CHIA PUDDING

Serves:        *2*
Prep Time:     *5*   Minutes

Cook Time:     *10*  Minutes

Total Time:    *15*  Minutes

## INGREDIENTS

- 5 tbs chia seeds
- 1 ½ tbs vanilla
- 2 tbs maple syrup
- 2 ½ cup almond milk
- 1 ½ cup strawberries
- 1 beet

## DIRECTIONS

1. Blend together the milk, strawberries, chopped beet, maple syrup, and vanilla
2. Pour into a cup and ad the chia
3. Stir every 5 minutes for 15 minutes
4. Refrigerate overnight
5. Serve topped with fruits

# BREAKFAST CASSEROLE

Serves:        **4**

Prep Time:    **10**   Minutes

Cook Time:    **35**   Minutes

Total Time:   **45**   Minutes

## INGREDIENTS

- 7 oz asparagus
- 3 tbs parsley
- 1 cup broccoli
- 1 zucchini
- 3 tbs oil
- 5 eggs
- Salt
- Pepper

## DIRECTIONS

1. Cook the diced zucchini, asparagus and broccoli florets in heated oil for about 5 minutes
2. Season with salt and pepper and remove from heat
3. Whisk the eggs and season then add the parsley
4. Place the vegetables in a greased pan then pour the eggs over
5. Bake in the preheated oven for about 35 minutes at 350F

# BLUEBERRY BALLS

Serves: **12**
Prep Time: **5** Minutes

Cook Time: **30** Minutes

Total Time: **35** Minutes

## INGREDIENTS

- 2 cups oats
- 1 cup blueberries
- 1/3 cup honey
- 1 tsp cinnamon
- 1 ½ tsp vanilla
- 1/3 cup almond butter

## DIRECTIONS

1. Mix the honey, vanilla, oats, almond butter, and cinnamon together
2. Fold in the blueberries
3. Refrigerate for at least 30 minutes
4. Form balls from the dough and serve

# ZUCCHINI BREAD

Serves:          *4*
Prep Time:    *10*   Minutes

Cook Time:    *40*   Minutes

Total Time:   *50*   Minutes

## INGREDIENTS

- 4 tbs honey
- 5 tbs oil
- 1 ½ tsp baking soda
- 3 eggs
- ½ cup walnuts
- 2 ½ cups flour
- 4 Medjool dates
- 1 banana
- 2 tsp mixed spice
- 1 ½ cup zucchini

## DIRECTIONS

1. Preheat the oven to 350 F
2. Chop the dates and the walnuts
3. Mix the flour, spice and baking soda together
4. Mix the eggs and banana in a food processor then add remaining ingredients and mix

5. Pour the batter into a pan and cook for at least 40 minutes
6. Allow to cool then serve

# BLUEBERRY PANCAKES

Serves: **4**

Prep Time: **10** Minutes

Cook Time: **20** Minutes

Total Time: **30** Minutes

## INGREDIENTS

- 1 cup whole wheat flour
- ¼ tsp baking soda
- ¼ tsp baking powder
- 1 cup blueberries
- 2 eggs
- 1 cup milk

## DIRECTIONS

1. In a bowl combine all ingredients together and mix well
2. In a skillet heat olive oil
3. Pour ¼ of the batter and cook each pancake for 1-2 minutes per side
4. When ready remove from heat and serve

Serves:          **4**
Prep Time:    **10**   Minutes

Cook Time:    **30**   Minutes

Total Time:    **40**   Minutes

## INGREDIENTS

- 1 cup whole wheat flour
- ¼ tsp baking soda
- ¼ tsp baking powder
- 1 cup nectarine
- 2 eggs
- 1 cup milk

## DIRECTIONS

1. In a bowl combine all ingredients together and mix well
2. In a skillet heat olive oil
3. Pour ¼ of the batter and cook each pancake for 1-2 minutes per side
4. When ready remove from heat and serve

# BANANA PANCAKES

Serves:       **4**
Prep Time:   **10**  Minutes
Cook Time:  **20**  Minutes
Total Time:  **30**  Minutes

## INGREDIENTS

- 1 cup whole wheat flour
- ¼ tsp baking soda
- ¼ tsp baking powder
- 1 cup mashed banana
- 2 eggs
- 1 cup milk

## DIRECTIONS

1. In a bowl combine all ingredients together and mix well
2. In a skillet heat olive oil
3. Pour ¼ of the batter and cook each pancake for 1-2 minutes per side
4. When ready remove from heat and serve

# ONION PANCAKES

Serves:        *4*
Prep Time:   *10*  Minutes

Cook Time:   *20*  Minutes

Total Time:  *30*  Minutes

## INGREDIENTS

- 1 cup whole wheat flour
- ¼ tsp baking soda
- ¼ tsp baking powder
- 1 cup onion
- 2 eggs
- 1 cup milk

## DIRECTIONS

1. In a bowl combine all ingredients together and mix well
2. In a skillet heat olive oil
3. Pour ¼ of the batter and cook each pancake for 1-2 minutes per side
4. When ready remove from heat and serve

# PANCAKES

Serves:        **4**

Prep Time:    **10**   Minutes

Cook Time:    **30**   Minutes

Total Time:    **40**   Minutes

## INGREDIENTS

- 1 cup whole wheat flour
- ¼ tsp baking soda
- ¼ tsp baking powder
- 2 eggs
- 1 cup milk

## DIRECTIONS

1. In a bowl combine all ingredients together and mix well
2. In a skillet heat olive oil
3. Pour ¼ of the batter and cook each pancake for 1-2 minutes per side
4. When ready remove from heat and serve

# RAISIN BREAKFAST MIX

Serves: **1**
Prep Time: **5** Minutes
Cook Time: **5** Minutes
Total Time: **10** Minutes

## INGREDIENTS

- ½ cup dried raisins
- ½ cup dried pecans
- ¼ cup almonds
- 1 cup coconut milk
- 1 tsp cinnamon

## DIRECTIONS

1. In a bowl combine all ingredients together
2. Serve with milk

# SAUSAGE BREAKFAST SANDWICH

Serves:        **2**

Prep Time:     **5**   Minutes

Cook Time:     **15**  Minutes

Total Time:    **20**  Minutes

## INGREDIENTS

- ¼ cup egg substitute
- 1 muffin
- 1 turkey sausage patty
- 1 tablespoon cheddar cheese

## DIRECTIONS

1. In a skillet pour egg and cook on low heat
2. Place turkey sausage patty in a pan and cook for 4-5 minutes per side
3. On a toasted muffin place the cooked egg, top with a sausage patty and cheddar cheese
4. Serve when ready

Serves:      **8-12**
Prep Time:   **10**   Minutes

Cook Time:   **20**   Minutes

Total Time:  **30**   Minutes

## INGREDIENTS

- 2 eggs
- 1 tablespoon olive oil
- 1 cup milk
- 2 cups whole wheat flour
- 1 tsp baking soda
- ¼ tsp baking soda
- 1 tsp cinnamon
- 1 cup strawberries

## DIRECTIONS

1. In a bowl combine all wet ingredients
2. In another bowl combine all dry ingredients
3. Combine wet and dry ingredients together
4. Pour mixture into 8-12 prepared muffin cups, fill 2/3 of the cups
5. Bake for 18-20 minutes at 375 F
6. When ready remove from the oven and serve

# DESSERTS

## BREAKFAST COOKIES

Serves:          **8-12**

Prep Time:       **5**    Minutes

Cook Time:       **15**   Minutes

Total Time:      **20**   Minutes

## INGREDIENTS

- 1 cup rolled oats
- ¼ cup applesauce
- ½ tsp vanilla extract
- 3 tablespoons chocolate chips
- 2 tablespoons dried fruits
- 1 tsp cinnamon

## DIRECTIONS

1. Preheat the oven to 325 F
2. In a bowl combine all ingredients together and mix well
3. Scoop cookies using an ice cream scoop
4. Place cookies onto a prepared baking sheet
5. Place in the oven for 12-15 minutes or until the cookies are done
6. When ready remove from the oven and serve

# PEAR TART

Serves:        **6-8**
Prep Time:     **25**    Minutes
Cook Time:     **25**    Minutes
Total Time:    **50**    Minutes

## INGREDIENTS

- 1 lb. pears
- 2 oz. brown sugar
- ½ lb. flaked almonds
- ¼ lb. porridge oat
- 2 oz. flour
- ¼ lb. almonds
- pastry sheets
- 2 tablespoons syrup

## DIRECTIONS

1. Preheat oven to 400 F, unfold pastry sheets and place them on a baking sheet
2. Toss together all ingredients together and mix well
3. Spread mixture in a single layer on the pastry sheets
4. Before baking decorate with your desired fruits
5. Bake at 400 F for 22-25 minutes or until golden brown
6. When ready remove from the oven and serve

# CARDAMOM TART

Serves: **6-8**

Prep Time: **25** Minutes

Cook Time: **25** Minutes

Total Time: **50** Minutes

## INGREDIENTS

- 4-5 pears
- 2 tablespoons lemon juice
- pastry sheets

## CARDAMOM FILLING

- ½ lb. butter
- ½ lb. brown sugar
- ½ lb. almonds
- ¼ lb. flour
- 1 ¼ tsp cardamom
- 2 eggs

## DIRECTIONS

1. Preheat oven to 400 F, unfold pastry sheets and place them on a baking sheet
2. Toss together all ingredients together and mix well
3. Spread mixture in a single layer on the pastry sheets
4. Before baking decorate with your desired fruits

5. Bake at 400 F for 22-25 minutes or until golden brown
6. When ready remove from the oven and serve

# APPLE TART

Serves:        *6-8*
Prep Time:     *25*   Minutes

Cook Time:     *25*   Minutes

Total Time:    *50*   Minutes


## INGREDIENTS

-   pastry sheets

## FILLING

-   1 tsp lemon juice
-   3 oz. brown sugar
-   1 lb. apples
-   150 ml double cream
-   2 eggs


## DIRECTIONS

1.  Preheat oven to 400 F, unfold pastry sheets and place them on a baking sheet
2.  Toss together all ingredients together and mix well
3.  Spread mixture in a single layer on the pastry sheets
4.  Before baking decorate with your desired fruits
5.  Bake at 400 F for 22-25 minutes or until golden brown
6.  When ready remove from the oven and serve

# CHOCHOLATE TART

Serves:        **6-8**

Prep Time:    **25**   Minutes

Cook Time:    **25**   Minutes

Total Time:   **50**   Minutes

## INGREDIENTS

- pastry sheets
- 1 tsp vanilla extract
- ½ lb. caramel
- ½ lb. black chocolate
- 4-5 tablespoons butter
- 3 eggs
- ¼ lb. brown sugar

## DIRECTIONS

1. Preheat oven to 400 F, unfold pastry sheets and place them on a baking sheet
2. Toss together all ingredients together and mix well
3. Spread mixture in a single layer on the pastry sheets
4. Before baking decorate with your desired fruits
5. Bake at 400 F for 22-25 minutes or until golden brown
6. When ready remove from the oven and serve

# OREO PIE

| | | |
|---|---|---|
| Serves: | *8-12* | |
| Prep Time: | *15* | Minutes |
| Cook Time: | *35* | Minutes |
| Total Time: | *50* | Minutes |

## INGREDIENTS

- pastry sheets
- 6-8 oz. chocolate crumb piecrust
- 1 cup half-and-half
- 1 package instant pudding mix
- 10-12 Oreo cookies
- 10 oz. whipped topping

## DIRECTIONS

1. Line a pie plate or pie form with pastry and cover the edges of the plate depending on your preference
2. In a bowl combine all pie ingredients together and mix well
3. Pour the mixture over the pastry
4. Bake at 400-425 F for 25-30 minutes or until golden brown
5. When ready remove from the oven and let it rest for 15 minutes

# SMOOTHIES AND DRINKS

## WATERMELON SMOOTHIE

Serves:         **1**
Prep Time:    **5**    Minutes

Cook Time:    **5**    Minutes

Total Time:   **10**   Minutes

### INGREDIENTS

- 4 cups watermelon
- 4-5 basil leaves
- 1 cup coconut water
- 1 cup ice

### DIRECTIONS

1. In a blender place all ingredients and blend until smooth
2. Pour smoothie in a glass and serve

# COCONUT SMOOTHIE

Serves:       *1*

Prep Time:    *5*   Minutes

Cook Time:    *5*   Minutes

Total Time:   *10*  Minutes

## INGREDIENTS

- 1 cup cherries
- 1 cup coconut water
- 1 tablespoon lime juice
- 2 tablespoons coconut flakes
- 1 cup cherries

## DIRECTIONS

1. In a blender place all ingredients and blend until smooth
2. Pour smoothie in a glass and serve

# AVOCADO SMOOTHIE

Serves:        **1**
Prep Time:     **5**   Minutes

Cook Time:     **5**   Minutes

Total Time:    **10**  Minutes

## INGREDIENTS

- 1 avocado
- 1 banana
- 1 cup soy milk
- 1 cup ice

## DIRECTIONS

1. In a blender place all ingredients and blend until smooth
2. Pour smoothie in a glass and serve

# GREEK SMOOTHIE

Serves:      **1**

Prep Time:   **5**   Minutes

Cook Time:   **5**   Minutes

Total Time:  **10**  Minutes

## INGREDIENTS

- 1 mango
- 3-4 tablespoons Greek yogurt
- 1 tsp cinnamon
- 1 cup ice

## DIRECTIONS

1. In a blender place all ingredients and blend until smooth
2. Pour smoothie in a glass and serve

# FRUIT SMOOTHIE

Serves:        *1*
Prep Time:     *5*   Minutes

Cook Time:     *5*   Minutes

Total Time:    *10*  Minutes

## INGREDIENTS

- 1 cup berries
- 4-5 oz. strawberry yogurt
- 1 cup cashew milk

## DIRECTIONS

1. In a blender place all ingredients and blend until smooth
2. Pour smoothie in a glass and serve

# PEANUT BUTTER SMOOTHIE

Serves:        *1*
Prep Time:   *5*   Minutes

Cook Time:   *5*   Minutes

Total Time:  *10*  Minutes

## INGREDIENTS

- 1 banana
- ¼ cup peanut butter
- 1 cup soy milk
- 1 cup ice

## DIRECTIONS

1. In a blender place all ingredients and blend until smooth
2. Pour smoothie in a glass and serve

# PINEAPPLE SMOOTHIE

Serves:          *1*

Prep Time:    5    Minutes

Cook Time:    5    Minutes

Total Time:   *10*   Minutes

## INGREDIENTS

- 2 cups pineapple
- ¼ cup mint leaves
- 1 cup coconut water
- 1 cup ice

## DIRECTIONS

1. In a blender place all ingredients and blend until smooth
2. Pour smoothie in a glass and serve

# BANANA & STRAWBERRY SMOOTHIE

Serves:        **1**
Prep Time:    **5**   Minutes

Cook Time:    **5**   Minutes

Total Time:   **10**  Minutes

## INGREDIENTS

- 4-5 strawberries
- 1 banana
- 1 cup almond milk

## DIRECTIONS

1. In a blender place all ingredients and blend until smooth
2. Pour smoothie in a glass and serve

# GREEN SMOOTHIE

Serves:        **1**
Prep Time:    **5**    Minutes

Cook Time:    **5**    Minutes

Total Time:   **10**   Minutes

## INGREDIENTS

- 1 cup baby spinach
- 1 cup coconut milk
- 1 cup pineapple
- 1 cup ice

## DIRECTIONS

1. **In a blender place all ingredients and blend until smooth**
2. **Pour smoothie in a glass and serve**

# BREAKFAST SMOOTHIE

Serves: **1**

Prep Time: **5** Minutes

Cook Time: **5** Minutes

Total Time: **10** Minutes

## INGREDIENTS

- 1 cup kale
- 1 cup almond milk
- 1 cup oats

## DIRECTIONS

1. In a blender place all ingredients and blend until smooth
2. Pour smoothie in a glass and serve

# FOURTH COOKBOOK

## ROASTED JALAPENO SOUP

Serves: **4**

Prep Time: **10** Minutes

Cook Time: **20** Minutes

Total Time: **30** Minutes

### INGREDIENTS

- 1 tablespoon olive oil
- 1 tablespoon roasted jalapeno
- ¼ red onion
- ½ cup all-purpose flour
- ¼ tsp salt
- ¼ tsp pepper
- 1 can vegetable broth
- 1 cup heavy cream

### DIRECTIONS

1. In a saucepan heat olive oil and sauté onion until tender
2. Add remaining ingredients to the saucepan and bring to a boil
3. When all the vegetables are tender transfer to a blender and blend until smooth
4. Pour soup into bowls, garnish with parsley and serve

# PARSNIP SOUP

Serves:        **4**

Prep Time:   **10**  Minutes

Cook Time:  **20**  Minutes

Total Time:  **30**  Minutes

## INGREDIENTS

- 1 tablespoon olive oil
- 1 cup parsnip
- ¼ red onion
- ½ cup all-purpose flour
- ¼ tsp salt
- ¼ tsp pepper
- 1 can vegetable broth
- 1 cup heavy cream

## DIRECTIONS

1. In a saucepan heat olive oil and sauté parsnip until tender
2. Add remaining ingredients to the saucepan and bring to a boil
3. When all the vegetables are tender transfer to a blender and blend until smooth
4. Pour soup into bowls, garnish with parsley and serve

# SPINACH SOUP

Serves: **4**
Prep Time: **10** Minutes
Cook Time: **20** Minutes
Total Time: **30** Minutes

## INGREDIENTS

- 1 tablespoon olive oil
- 1 lb. spinach
- ¼ red onion
- ½ cup all-purpose flour
- ¼ tsp salt
- ¼ tsp pepper
- 1 can vegetable broth
- 1 cup heavy cream

## DIRECTIONS

1. In a saucepan heat olive oil and sauté spinach until tender
2. Add remaining ingredients to the saucepan and bring to a boil
3. When all the vegetables are tender transfer to a blender and blend until smooth
4. Pour soup into bowls, garnish with parsley and serve

# CUCUMBER SOUP

Serves: **4**

Prep Time: **10** Minutes

Cook Time: **20** Minutes

Total Time: **30** Minutes

## INGREDIENTS

- 1 tablespoon olive oil
- 1 lb. cucumber
- ¼ red onion
- ½ cup all-purpose flour
- ¼ tsp salt
- ¼ tsp pepper
- 1 can vegetable broth
- 1 cup heavy cream

## DIRECTIONS

1. In a saucepan heat olive oil and sauté onion until tender
2. Add remaining ingredients to the saucepan and bring to a boil
3. When all the vegetables are tender transfer to a blender and blend until smooth
4. Pour soup into bowls, garnish with parsley and serve

# SWEETCORN SOUP

Serves:        **4**
Prep Time:    **10**  Minutes

Cook Time:    **20**  Minutes

Total Time:   **30**  Minutes

## INGREDIENTS

- 1 tablespoon olive oil
- 1 lb. sweetcorn
- ¼ red onion
- ½ cup all-purpose flour
- ¼ tsp salt
- ¼ tsp pepper
- 1 can vegetable broth
- 1 cup heavy cream

## DIRECTIONS

1. In a saucepan heat olive oil and sauté onion until tender
2. Add remaining ingredients to the saucepan and bring to a boil
3. When all the vegetables are tender transfer to a blender and blend until smooth
4. Pour soup into bowls, garnish with parsley and serve

CPSIA information can be obtained
at www.ICGtesting.com
Printed in the USA
BVHW071351040321
601713BV00003B/292